EXISTENTIALISM AND MODERN LITERATURE

EXISTENTIALISM
AND
MODERN LITERATURE

AN ESSAY IN EXISTENTIAL CRITICISM

by

DAVIS DUNBAR McELROY, Ph.D.

PHILOSOPHICAL LIBRARY
New York

Printed in the United States of America

By all means let us take life seriously, but let us be serious about things that matter.

Douglas, South Wind

CONTENTS

ACKNOWLEDGMENTS

The following authors and publishers have kindly permitted me to use copyright material: William Barrett, *What is Existentialism?* (Partisan Review, Series 2, copyright 1947); Van Wyck Brooks, *The Writer in America* (E. P. Dutton and Co., copyright 1953); T. S. Eliot, "The Hollow Men" from *The Collected Poems of T. S. Eliot* (Harcourt, Brace and World, Inc., copyright 1936), *The Cocktail Party* (Harcourt, Brace and World, Inc., copyright 1950), *The Confidential Clerk* (Harcourt, Brace and World, Inc., copyright 1954); William Faulkner, *A Fable* (Random House Inc., copyright 1954); Erich Fromm, *The Escape From Freedom* (Holt, Rinehart and Winston, Inc., copyright 1941), *Man for Himself* (Holt, Rinehart and Winston, Inc., copyright 1947); Ortega y Gasset, *The Revolt of the Masses* (W. W. Norton, copyright 1932); Vyacheslav Ivanov, *Freedom and the Tragic Life*, translated by Norman Cameron (Farrar, Straus and Cudahy, Inc., copyright 1960); Thomas Mann, Introduction to Franz Kafka's *The Castle*, translated by Edwin and Willa Muir (Alfred A. Knopf, copyright 1949); Arthur Miller, *Death of a Salesman* (Viking Press, copyright 1949).

PREFACE

The three parts of this small book were originally written as lectures. In preparing them I paraphrased and quoted freely from the best material I could find. Unfortunately I did not document my sources in the usual way because at that time I had no idea that the talks would ever be published. I have tried as best I could to indicate those to whom I am indebted. If I have left any debt unacknowledged I am sorry. I can say with complete truthfulness that I had no intention of plagiarizing but of presenting the existentialistic view of man as clearly and as persuasively as possible.

Just one word more. I have used the word "God" in a number of places and I would like to explain what I understood by the word when I wrote it. Spinoza's concept of God as the sum of all the natural forces which rule the universe and of the phenomena which result from them has given me the greatest satisfaction. In Spinoza's sense, God governs man from within by making each of us a unique experiment in humanity. You and I are not only different from one another, we are different from every man who ever lived, or ever will live; just as every snowflake is different from every other snowflake which has ever fallen, or ever will fall. The destiny of mankind lies in these individual differences, and in the potential good they bear. The truth of every man is the good within him; his greatest chance for happiness and satisfaction is to seek out and to become this good. When he does this, he becomes one with God, as the Christians say.

INTRODUCTION

Existentialism has been with us for a good while now, and yet one still hears people asking What is Existentialism? What they seem to want is a simple definition in one or two sentences. Despite one's best efforts, it is impossible to reduce it to this. One may as well try to explain human existence in a single sentence, for human existence is the subject matter with which the existentialists deal. Still, it is rather discouraging not to be able to give these earnest and, let us be candid, rather mindless questioners the simple answer they are seeking. The best advice you can give them is that they must seek the answer in the writings of the existentialists for themselves.

Even at the source, however, something of the same perplexity exists. In one of his lectures, the Catholic existentialist Gabriel Marcel told his audience that

> . . . not a day passes without someone (generally a woman of culture, but perhaps a janitor or a streetcar conductor) asking me what existentialism is. No one will be surprised that I evade the question. I reply that it is too difficult or too long to explain: all one can do is try to elucidate a key-notion of it, not to formulate a definition.[1]

If the existentialists themselves find it difficult to explain what they are up to, I am bound to come to grief. Nevertheless I feel obliged to do my best to "elucidate a key-notion of it," as Marcel put it. For my purpose I have chosen a key-notion suggested by the word "existentialism" itself; that is, the problem of man's existence.

1. Reinhardt, *The Existentialist Revolt,* page 22.

THE PROBLEM OF MAN'S EXISTENCE

A very pretty Roman myth makes an admirable beginning for our inquiries. One day, the story goes, when Care was crossing a river, she noticed some clay on the bank. She took up a piece and began to fashion it. While she was still reflecting on what she had fashioned, Jupiter arrived on the scene. Care asked him to give this form of clay a soul, which Jupiter promptly did. But then a dispute arose between Care and Jupiter: each wanted to give his own name to the new creature. And while they were still arguing, Earth came along and insisted that her name be given to the creature, since it was she who had provided it with a body. The three thereupon called in Saturn to judge their dispute. "Jupiter," said Saturn, "since you have given this thing a soul, you shall receive this creature after its death; you, Earth, shall in the end receive its body; but since Care first shaped this creature, *she shall possess it as long as it lives.* And as for the creature's name, let it be called man *(homo),* since it has been fashioned out of earth *(humo.)*"[1]

As seen in the context of this myth, man is a composite of care and clay; for we must suppose that Care, in fashioning man, compounded something in his very nature which causes him to be unremittingly anxious about himself. In other words man is a creature who suffers from needless worries, from unreasonable doubts, and from causeless fears — and he does this because it is in his very nature to do so, because he is man. As I shall soon make clear, this myth has touched the heart of the problem of human existence. However, it will be necessary to examine it from

1. William Barrett, *What is Existentialism?*, page 32.

1

several points of view before we begin to fully understand what it means.

Let us begin by comparing the myth with one of the more recent ones being propagated by psychoanalysis. "To be born," says Otto Rank, "is to be cast out of the Garden of Eden." According to Rank, before he is born, man lives in a state of bliss. But, with the exception of his death, man's birth is the most painfully anxious experience which he undergoes. "The experience of being born causes a profound shock to the helpless organism; a shock which involves not only physical separation from the mother, but also physiological hazards and changes of state. This painful experience sets up or carries with it the first and most fundamental feeling of anxiety which the individual ever experiences. Rank calls it the 'primal anxiety.'"

For Rank, this "primal anxiety" is the source of all the anxieties of death, doubt, and guilt which perplex man throughout his painful existence. But he goes even further: he states that "not only all socially valuable creations of man, but even the fact of becoming man, arise from a specific reaction to the experience of his birth."[1]

In the mythology of psychoanalysis, Care has been reduced from the role of artist to that of midwife, but her function is still about the same. In issuing man into the world, Care has given him that doubtful blessing, or that painful burden, which accounts for his humanity — that is, his ceaseless and unrelenting anxiety.

"Life is a dark saying," wrote Kierkegaard, the great prophet of existentialism, and perhaps there is some reason to agree with him. To Christians, however, all of this should seem familiar enough, for it contains many elements of the Christian concept of original sin. For this reason, I do not believe that many readers will find it at all surprising when I say that man, who is plagued by the constant uneasiness of anxiety, and by the dread which comes from causeless fears, is also the victim of a nameless guilt,

1. Patrick Mullahy, *Oedipus Myth and Complex*, page 162.

for Christianity long ago traced the primordial source of this guilt in the story of the Fall.

According to the Christian myth, when Adam ate the fruit from the tree of knowledge, he brought upon himself the curse of consciousness, that he should know evil as well as good — and particularly the evil of his own death. That the result of this knowledge was disastrous we all know far too well. In the Garden, Adam and Eve lived an idyllic existence. There was harmony between them; they had little to do; and they experienced none of the doubts, fears, and anguish which no man has escaped since their tragic error. In other words, they were as much a part of nature as small children and other animals. But, properly speaking, they were not yet human, and although their first free act of choice was unfortunate, to say the least, it was also a sign that they were emerging from the unconscious existence of the pre-human. Their action against divine authority, their sin, was also the first act of human freedom, the first human act. But the curse of this new freedom was that although man was still bound to nature by his body, his new-found consciousness was no longer limited to the unreflecting awareness with which nature goes about her work.

The preceding interpretation of the Fall, and a great deal more, I owe to Erich Fromm, who has brought me more than any other writer to view man from the existential point of view. In *Man for Himself*, Fromm explains that "man's self-awareness, reason, and imagination have disrupted the harmony which characterizes animal existence, and their emergence has made man into an anomaly, into the freak of the universe. He is a part of nature, subject to her physical laws and unable to change them, yet he transcends the rest of nature. He is set apart while being a part; he is homeless, yet chained to the home he shares with all creatures. Cast into this world at an accidental place and time, he is forced out of it, again accidentally. Being aware of himself, he realizes his powerlessness and the limitations of his existence. He even visualizes his own end: death. Never is he free from the dichotomy of his existence: he cannot rid himself of his mind, even if he should want to; he cannot rid himself of his

3

body as long as he is alive—and his body makes him want to be alive."[1]

Fromm goes on to say that man's reason is both a blessing and a curse, because it drives him to attempt to solve the insoluble dichotomy of his own existence. Man, in other words, is the only animal for whom existence is a problem which he has to solve and from which he cannot escape, for a man's life cannot be lived by repeating the pattern of his species by instinct, each individual must make his own life. As Kierkegaard points out, "being a man is not like being an animal, for in man the individual is more than the species."[2] Nor can man go back to the pre-human, even if he wanted to: he must go ahead and develop his reason until he becomes master of nature and of himself.

Nevertheless "every stage man reaches leaves him discontented and perplexed, and this very perplexity urges him to move toward new solutions. There is no innate drive for progress in man; it is the contradiction in his own existence that makes him proceed on the way he set out. Having lost Paradise, the unity with nature, he has become the eternal wanderer (Odysseus, Oedipus, Abraham, Faust); he is impelled to go forward and with everlasting effort to make the unknown known by filling in with answers the blank spaces of his knowledge. He is driven to overcome this inner split, tormented by a craving for absoluteness, for another kind of harmony which can lift the curse by which he was separated from nature, from his fellow men, and from himself. He feels impelled to give a final account of himself to himself, and to explain in absolute terms the meaning of his existence."[3] But as long as man remains what he is, his search for absolutes will be fruitless.

If we are to believe Sartre and a number of other existentialists, man's inability to reduce human existence to absolutes

1. Erich Fromm, *Man for Himself*, page 40 f.
2. Kierkegaard, *Sickness Unto Death*, page 198, note.
3. Erich Fromm, *Man for Himself*, page 41 and note. Curiously enough at the time Fromm wrote this he was not only unaware of his spiritual and intellectual kinship with the existentialists, he was openly antagonistic toward them.

is ontological. Nor is the idea a novel one: as far back as St. Thomas Aquinas and perhaps even further one catches glimpses of it. St. Thomas, it will be remembered, based his entire ontology on three principles, one of which was that "a thing cannot 'be' and 'not be' at one and the same time;" Sartre's major philosophical work bears the title *Being and Nothingness.*

The existentialistic explanation runs something like this: with every apprehension of being, man also apprehends the possibility or "threat" of non-being. In other words, when an individual consciousness becomes aware of the presence or existence of something other than itself, something which exists outside and independently of itself, it is also aware of the possibility that that thing may someday cease to exist. And this threat of non-being is not confined to objects which are external to the individual consciousness. When such a consciousness becomes aware of its own existence as a being, it also becomes aware of the threat of non-being to that existence.

From what has gone before, I expect no one is going to be much surprised to learn that this threat of non-being puts man in a state of basal anxiety. Man is anxious because he is agonizingly aware of the threat of annihilation to his precious individuality, a threat from which there is no final and positive escape except death, the thing he most fears. Paul Tillich considers this state of anxiety to be the basic human predicament: he calls it the anxiety of fate and death. But our basic state of anxiety, according to Tillich, does not cause us anguish merely on the issues of fate and death. We also suffer from the anxiety of doubt and meaninglessness: which is to say, the threat of non-being to all our beliefs and ideas. And, as a final blow, our apprehensions of the threat of non-being to the results of all our actions creates in us an anxiety of guilt and condemnation.[1]

Now all this seems harmless enough. Where, then, do the difficulties and the risks to one's peace of mind come in?

I would like the reader to consider, if he will, that what I have just said means precisely this: that physically, intellectually,

1. Paul Tillich, *The Courage to Be*, passim.

morally, and spiritually he is forever standing on a quaking bog; and if he makes one heavy step, he will be instantly engulfed in the quicksand of despair. But even if he escapes, he is never on solid ground. The thing that makes him human is the very thing that makes him uneasy in his existence, for the first fact of his existence, as we have seen in myth and in metaphysics, is his care, his anxiety, his dread, and his guilt.

Nor can he escape by anticipating the death he either dreads or longs for, for death implies the loss of his individuality, or self, and it is this dread of lost self (the threat of non-being to the uniqueness of the individual) which is close to the center of the problem of man's uneasy existence. In fact this loss of self is the greatest calamity which can befall the individual, because only the man who is completely and authentically himself can be said to be truly alive.

But this seems to start a paradox, for an existential appraisal of man in the modern world reveals that a great part of humanity cannot properly be said to be alive at all, they merely exist. And this arises from the fact that they have no true individuality; they have, in other words, no self which they could lose. And so far are they from desiring the self which they have never had, they fear it and flee in all directions in their endeavors to escape it. But if the loss of self is the greatest calamity that can befall an individual, how is it that so many men try desperately to escape the self?

The answer seems to be that while it is true that men fear death, and dread the loss of self which death implies, there is a more basic fear, the fear of life itself. As Otto Rank says, the memory of his painful physical separation from the mother at birth fills the individual with a dread of further separation whether it be physical or psychical. Thus, even the dread of death is based upon the fear of life, because death, in this respect, is the final fact of complete separation.

In *The Escape from Freedom* Erich Fromm explains how man's isolation has been increased by his loss of primal ties with nature, family, tribe, and religion, ties which formerly protected him from the most awful human predicament, complete aloneness.

But we have now reached the stage, Fromm says, when the only way we can live authentically is by overcoming this loneliness by being completely ourselves. According to Fromm we must intensify our physical and psychical separation, not try to lessen it or escape it, for modern man, in Sartre's phrase, is condemned to be free. But the thesis of Fromm's book is that because of our feeling of insignificance, powerlessness, and hopelessness, we are trying to escape from this freedom.

At this point, perhaps I should attempt to clarify what I mean by freedom, for it is a concept which will become of increasing importance as I continue. Jean-Paul Sartre, an incomparable maker of phrases, tells us that "man *is* his freedom," and it would be well, I think, for all of us to know exactly what kind of freedom he has in mind.

Once again I turned to Erich Fromm to clear this matter up. Fromm points out that there are two kinds of freedom: "freedom from," and "freedom to." What is meant by "freedom to do something" we all understand very well — particularly if it is something we would like to do but cannot afford. In fact most of us wish that we had more of it. "Freedom from," however, needs some explanation; because, being free in this particular way, we tend to take it for granted. This "freedom from" is the kind of freedom which animals, small children, and primitive men do not have; and they do not have it because they are ruled by external compulsions over which they have no control. But, as man approaches maturity, he gradually frees himself from instinctive and compulsory behavior and he develops his powers of self-reliance and of choice. He is not, of course, free to do everything which comes into his head (as most people immediately assume you to mean when you say that man is free.) On the contrary, he is free in the way of man: he is free from the strict necessity of submitting to a compulsory, limited, and irreversible course of action.

The development of individual freedom reached a high point in the West during the latter part of the nineteenth century with the ideal, never fully realized, of democratic liberalism. Perhaps it would be well for me to remind the reader of the nature of

7

that ideal, for most of us have come to maturity in a world in which it no longer exists. I greatly admire Ortega y Gassett's description of it:[1]

> The political doctrine which has represented the loftiest endeavour towards common life is liberal democracy. It carries to the extreme the determination to have consideration for one's neighbor. Liberalism is that principle of political rights, according to which the public authority, in spite of being all-powerful, limits itself and attempts, even at its own expense, to leave room in the state over which it rules, for those to live who neither think nor feel as it does, that is to say, as do the stronger, the majority. Liberalism — it is well to recall this today — is the supreme form of generosity; it is the right which the majority concedes to minorities and hence it is the noblest cry that has ever resounded on this planet. It announces the determination to share existence with the enemy; more than that, with an enemy which is weak. It was incredible that the human species should have arrived at so noble an attitude, so paradoxical, so refined, so acrobatic, so anti-natural. Hence, it is not to be wondered at that this same humanity should soon appear anxious to get rid of it. It is a discipline too difficult and complex to take firm root on earth.

But this is only one side of the picture. On the other we find that the very thing which made individual freedom a possibility — the mechanization of the means of production, a competitive economic system, and democracy — has tended more and more to force man into that state of complete isolation which he fears so greatly. The result has been that modern man has become a cog in a vast machine, and he is made to work for inhuman ends. He has become, as we all know (whether we admit it is another matter), a servant to the very machine he has built. Economic crises, unemployment, and war govern his fate. The world he has built has become his master; the work of his own hands has become a god before whom he bows down. Is it any wonder,

---

1. Ortega y Gassett, *Revolt of the Masses*, page 83.

then, that modern man, who has so much more than ever before, should be haunted by a feeling of isolation, of insignificance, and of powerlessness?

But this is by no means all. In casting off his primary ties, in liberating himself, modern Western man has lost his God. This, perhaps, is the real tragedy, for had he still God to look to, man could bear to live and even hope in the Waste Land of the modern world. But the awful truth is this — and if you do not recognize it you know very little about your fellows — for many people now living, God is dead. As a consequence, freedom has become an intolerable burden to modern man; he can no longer stand his isolation, and he feels he must somehow devise means to reverse, to escape, or to improve his situation.

At first glance, it would seem that there are three possibilities open to modern man:

1. to return to the primary ties of nature, clan, and religion which supported him in the past.
2. to escape from the burden of his freedom to *new* dependencies and states of submissiveness.
3. to advance to a more positive freedom which is based upon the uniqueness and individuality of man.

Of these three, however, one possibility is closed to him — *he cannot go back*. Modern man has reached the point of no return, for once the primary ties are broken, they cannot be reestablished, no more than any of us can return to the blissful prenatal existence of the womb.

But modern man can, and does, seek every avenue of escape from the burden of his freedom and the obligation to be as himself. He can, for example, narcotize his feeling of isolation, insignificance, and powerlessness; his anxieties of death, doubt, and guilt. When an individual resorts to drugs, alcohol, food, sex, work, social activities, sports, entertainment, and intellectual activity not for the pleasures which they afford, but for the purpose of numbing his sensibilities, he does so because he desires to escape his anxieties. We all know these fugitives from selfhood; they are the people who inhabit T. S. Eliot's *Waste*

9

Land and his other poems. But these roads of escape are merely the most obvious and the most easily observed.

Post-Freudian psychoanalysis, notably the work of Erich Fromm, has discovered what the human psyche will do, and is doing, in its attempts to escape the burden of its freedom and its anxieties. Fromm has gone so far as to state that most of the problems facing the psychoanalyst today are problems of personality — problems of inauthentic existence on the part of the patient — and not problems which involve only the subconscious and its psychological manifestations. Among the numerous mechanisms of escape by which his patients have vainly endeavored to submerge and to frustrate their existence as unique and self-determining individuals, five which Dr. Fromm lists are worthy of special attention. The five are masochism, sadism, destructiveness, authoritarianism, and automaton conformity. Inasmuch as all arise either from feelings of isolation, of insignificance, or of powerlessness, the things we can look for in these mechanisms of escape are the need for submission, the need for self-importance, or the lust for power.

The masochist, for example, seeks to escape his anxiety through submitting himself to a powerful and arbitrary person or institution which rules and even torments him mentally and physically. His suffering gives him a sense of security because he feels, in his torment, that he is no longer isolated and so he enjoys his pain. The sadist, on the other hand, in order to dispel his feelings of weakness and isolation, must find a victim, a person whom he can completely dominate, and upon whom he can inflict mental and physical discomfort, even torture. His essential weakness can be detected in his dependence upon his victim. As long as his victim is submissive, the sadist feels secure; but if the victim should resist, or escape, the realization of his insignificance and weakness leaves the sadist as anxious as before.

Destructiveness is an element in all five mechanisms, for all five are essentially directed at the destruction of the individual self. In this sense, it might be well to observe that this self-directed destructiveness is the outcome of unlived life; that is, it is precisely because he lacks the courage to live completely and convincingly as himself, that the person who relies upon one of these mechanisms of escape seeks to destroy his individuality or self. As a mechanism of escape, however, destructiveness assumes another form.

The destructive person attempts to remove his anxieties of isolation and powerlessness by removing the cause of them by violence. This violence can be directed against either persons or things. When there is a shortage of food, the destructive individual's first impulse is to smash and burn a bakery or a food store, and this impulse is not motivated by the expectation of loot, but by a need to remove the cause of his anxiety. Such an act of violence gives the destructive man a fleeting but necessary feeling of power. The United States, it seems to me, is indulging in this escape mechanism on a national scale in its efforts to seek out and destroy its native communists. But it should be fairly obvious, I think, that the sacrifice of a handful of scapegoats is not going to give us the security which we so desperately need, for the true source of our anxiety lies elsewhere. Meanwhile, there is more than a slight chance that, as a people, we might resort to authoritarianism, an escape mechanism which has been growing in popularity since the first World War.

The person who seeks to escape his anxieties through authoritarianism hungers to submit himself to an irrational authority, and such an authority must have complete and absolute control over him, and it must be beyond criticism. The authoritarian character finds inner security by becoming part of this authority which he believes to be greater and more powerful than himself, and as long as he is a part of the authority he feels that he is participating in the authority's strength. To be rejected by the authority, on the other hand, means to be thrown into a void, to face the horror of his own nothingness. Anything, to the authoritarian character, is better than this. He wishes to be loved and approved by the authority, but even punishment by it is better than rejection. The sincere supporters of Nazism, of Fascism, and of Communism are the very type of the authoritarian character; and this is the source, too, of their willingness, their eager-

11

ness, to "confess" their "crimes" against the authority which then destroys them. But this is not the only form of authoritarianism.

The usual form for an irrational authority to assume is that of a hierarchy of elite such as existed in pre-war Germany and Italy, and which still exists in Russia. But there is such a thing as an anonymous authority which exhibits all the characteristics which I have mentioned before in connection with irrational authority. Such an authority comes into being whenever large numbers of the citizens of a democracy seek to escape the uncertainty of their existence by resorting to automaton conformity. The mechanism of automaton conformity is invoked whenever one adopts entirely the kind of personality offered him by cultural patterns; in short, by becoming exactly as all others are and as they expect their fellows to be. The automaton conformist wipes out, or attempts to wipe out, the difference between himself and others, thus overcoming his fear of solitude and powerlessness. Such a person aims to think, feel, imagine, and act exactly like all others of his culture or class. Thus neither his ideas, his desires, his emotions, nor his personality are properly his own. What he has done, incredible as it may seem, is to substitute a pseudo-self for his real self.

But the automaton conformist goes a bit further. His destructiveness does not stop with himself, but is extended to anyone who reminds him of his loss of individuality — he cannot stand non-conformity. In his book on the mass-man, perhaps the best portrait of the automaton conformist ever written, Ortega y Gassett describes what this mechanism of escape leads to:[1]

> Nothing indicates more clearly the characteristic of the day than the fact that there are so few countries where an opposition exists. In almost all, a homogeneous mass weighs on public authority and crushes down, annihilates every opposing group. And this mass does not wish to share life with those who are not of it. It has a deadly hatred of all that is not itself. The mass says to itself, "L'etat, c'est moi," which is a complete mistake. The state is the mass only in the sense

1. Ortega y Gassett, *Revolt of the Masses,* page 132.

12

in which it can be said of two men that they are identical because neither of them is named John. The contemporary state and the mass coincide only in being anonymous. But the mass-man does in fact believe that he is the state, and he will tend more and more to set its machinery working on whatsoever pretext, to crush beneath it any creative minority which disturbs it — disturbs it in any order of things, in politics, in ideas, in industry.

The portrait of modern man — that is, of ourselves — is now all but complete. Alone, afraid, and condemned to our freedom; victims of a nameless anxiety, dread, anguish, and guilt; we either kiss the hand that scourges us, or visit unspeakable horrors on others — witness Dachau, Hiroshima, and the Soviet slave-labor camps. Or we strive to lose our identity by submerging our God-given individuality in the featureless mass of anonymous humanity; or we drown it in dope, lust, or senseless activity. And our destructiveness is as pervasive as our despair. Lacking faith, charity, and even pity, we are constant in just one thing — violence.

Our violence is everywhere: not just in our streets, in our homes, in our everyday lives; it is in our hearts, in our minds, and in our souls. We do not really fear the Bomb, we lovers of violence, we worship it, and we secretly yearn for the day when we can destroy the world and ourselves in a great blissful flash of unholy consummation.

But despite our best, or our worst, efforts we are bound to fail in our attempts to destroy ourselves. Our debasement, our degradation, is simply the result of our refusal to realize completely and legitimately the potentialities of our freedom and of ourselves. We will fail because our genuine self does not die. It is changed into an accusing shadow, a phantom which constantly reminds us of the inferiority of the life we live compared with the one we ought to be living. Even a debased man survives his self-inflicted destruction.

Erich Fromm has told us that what man must do, and what he will eventually do if he survives the holocaust which is to come, is to avail himself of the third alternative which is open to him. "Eventually man must face the truth about himself: it is the only genuine solution. He must acknowledge his fundamental aloneness and solitude in a universe indifferent to his fate; he must recognize that there is no transcendent power which can solve his problem for him. He must do this because he cannot escape his responsibility for himself and the fact that only by using his own powers can he give meaning to his life. But meaning does not imply certainty: indeed, the quest for certainty blocks the search for meaning, for it is uncertainty which impels man to unfold his powers. Man will never cease to be perplexed, to wonder, and to raise new questions, not as long as he remains in his present form. But if he faces the truth without panic, he will recognize that there is no meaning to life except the meaning a man gives his life by unfolding of his powers, by living productively. Only constant vigilance, activity, and effort can keep him from failing in the one task that matters— the full development of his powers within the limitations set by the laws of his existence. Only if man recognizes the human situation, the dichotomies inherent in his existence and his capacity to unfold his powers, will he be able to succeed in his task: which is to be himself and to achieve happiness by the full realization of those faculties which are peculiarly his — the powers of reason, faith, and productive work."[1]

1. Erich Fromm, *Man for Himself*, pages 44-45.

MODERN LITERATURE: A WARNING

In the preceding section I have attempted to convey some impression of the existentialistic view of the problem of man's existence. I will not attempt to deny that this view is a rather unpleasant one, nor will I deny that it is disruptive, unharmonious, rather dismal, and, when contrasted to the more optimistic view which has prevailed for about two hundred years in the West, somewhat corrupt. But whatever it is, we cannot pretend to be ignorant of its existence nor of its results for modern art is largely a reflection of it, and the unharmonious, corrupt, dismal, and shattering effect of much of our painting, music, and literature can be traced to it.

In painting, for example, the revolution in technique which began with Turner, and which was accelerated by the impressionists, has long since run its course. Aside from their bold experiments with light, however, the impressionists accepted and maintained the traditions of Western European painting. It is for this reason that we tend to regard the uproar that their paintings first created as superfluous and silly. But the impressionistic movement was immediately followed by a revolution in the total approach to art, and the disorder which it has created we do not find so amusing. The artistic ideal, the standards, the intellectual attitudes, and the moral preconceptions of the surrealists, for example, mark a radical change from the Western tradition. In its most extreme form, Dada, this revolution took on the form of artistic nihilism, and it may be described as a deliberate attempt to shatter all that is known or knowable in and through art. Of course there were artists in the movement who had a very good reason for adopting this violent method: the first World War was proof enough that all was not going so well under the received impression that mankind was on the road to perfection. But at the same time, the extreme radicalism of the movement justifies a few querulous complaints from the spectator who is still suffering from the notion that order has a place in art.

But the dadaists and surrealists were not the only ones to create confusion in artistic matters: Picasso, the cubists, and the abstractionists have all contributed their share by attempting to give us new powers of vision through the spacial distortions which mark their compositions. And throughout the paintings of all these various schools, we find these consistent themes: man degraded, man in peril, man without faith, man without hope, mercy, charity, love — in short, man who is scarcely recognizable as man at all. In fact many modern artists seem to avoid man as a subject for their paintings whenever they can; or, when they cannot, to choose for their human subjects the clown, the judge, or the hangman — three figures who are scarcely human at all. But these things need not be enlarged upon: it is sufficient to make a single visit to a gallery of modern painting to gather the overwhelming impression that the world has run mad.

But such an impression is by no means confined to one's contacts with painting. In music we find a similar disruption of form, of traditional devices, and of traditional aims and ideals. The cacophony and formlessness of jazz is paralleled by similar tendencies in more serious and ambitious pieces; and in both realms, sounds and rhythms have become deliberately violent and unpleasant. The result of this is that whereas each had its adherents in the past, at the present time there is little quarrel between the admirers of bebop and, say, those who admire Bartok. If you can stand rock and roll, you can stand Bartok's boiler-factory effects, for both have been afflicted by the same disruptive forces, and with strikingly similar results; consequently the jazz and serious music of today are executed very nearly upon the same plane of achievement and with the same ends in view. It has been widely recognized, in fact, that our music, and its adjunct, the ballet, were among the first art forms to catch the perverse rhythms of modern life and rather unhappy condition of man which these rhythms have created.

But it is when we turn to literature that we find inescapable proof that the existentialists are not alone in regarding man as living a desperate and perilous existence in the modern world. And perhaps the most surprising thing about all this is that despite the fact that Americans are generally regarded, and regard themselves, as being the most optimistic people on earth, and as living full and rewarding lives, it is such American authors as James T. Farrell, John Steinbeck, John Dos Passos, Arthur Miller, Tennessee Williams, and, above all, William Faulkner, who paint modern life in its darkest colors. Nothing as stark and as full of degradation and corruption as Faulkner's work has come from abroad. Nothing as full of despair has been seen in the theaters of Europe as Arthur Miller's *The Death of a Salesman.* It may be, of course, that these American authors are merely capitalizing on sensationalism. But it is significant, I think, that European authors, who are certainly not above a bit of pandering to public taste when it pays, can conceive of no character as consummately evil as Faulkner's Popeye, nor as universally superfluous to himself and to the world as Willy Loman, the salesman in Miller's play. Poor old Willy! He was so accustomed to regarding himself as a commodity that when his shoeshine and his smile began to grow dull, he so depreciated in value, even to himself, that he merely discarded himself by piling up his automobile, a symbolic form of suicide. William Saroyan once observed about America that "nowhere in the world is there so much junk." F. Scott Fitzgerald's major creation, Gatsby, a character in a novel which is celebrated by our influential critics, revealed the shoddiness of the American dream as it appeared during the "gay twenties." Hemingway, who tried to outlive his despair by sheer bravado, proved that swagger is no cure for spiritual bankruptcy when he blew his head off.

We can go back even further and detect a somber note in American writing. A hundred years ago, that imperturbable American Hesiod, Henry Thoreau, observed that most of the men

17

about him lived "lives of quiet desperation." And Ishmael, the sole survivor of the cataclysm which closes that great epic of pessimism, *Moby Dick,* saves himself by clinging to a floating coffin. I mention these things in passing, for I take them to mean that our artists, at least, are not unaware of the things of which I spoke in my opening section.

I believe it is time, now, to decide just how seriously we should regard these rather unpleasant elements in our art and our literature. We can assume, I believe, that the things which I have just described actually exist, and that the artists who have produced the works in which they appear were not oblivious to them — in other words, they knew what they were doing, and probably why they were doing it. If the reader has any doubts as to the validity of this statement, I take it to be an indication of just one thing: that he hasn't come into contact with the same examples of modern art, music, or literature that I have. Which observation should serve to remind us that it is perfectly possible to be acquainted with an appreciable amount of modern artistic production without becoming consciously aware of its existential elements. In other words, not all painting, composing, or writing today is done from the point of view which I have been stressing. Some of it, a great deal in fact, is wholesome, normal, confident, and well within the bounds of the artistic proprieties which tradition has established.

The view of man which is assumed in this traditional art is one that is familiar to us all. Man is shown with faults, certainly, but not as perpetually damned for them — he has some hope for salvation. But in his earthly existence, he finds, as did Faust, that even at the peril of his immortal soul he cannot make the pleasures o'erweigh the pangs of human existence. Like Faust, however, he ultimately finds the satisfaction for which he seeks in productive work — he has, therefore, some chance for contentment. In his service and his love for others, and in their love for him, he can escape the anxiety of his existence as an isolated and insignificant being — in other words he has some chance for happiness.

In considering this noble view of man, we seem to re-emerge

into the bright sunlight after wandering through some gloomy and oppressive jungle. As far as I am concerned, there is no question as to which view I prefer. But I think that we still must decide which is the most significant, which is the most meaningful, which is the truest representation of man's position in the modern world. As for myself, I would choose to walk in the sunlight of that ideal of manhood were it not that, like Hamlet, I have bad dreams. Dachau, Hiroshima, and the Soviet slave-labor camps; the stink of burning human flesh; the horror of thousands of seared, featureless, and sightless upturned faces; the thought of men turned into animals without minds or souls — these things make for a somewhat troubled sleep. I would like to believe in the noble view, but I cannot; something has been left out, the view is incomplete.

I believe it is true that man can be saved, that he can find contentment, and that he will find that happiness which love will bring him — but only if he is true to himself, and he is anything but this. According to Vyacheslav Ivanov, a student of Dostoevsky's works, "the question of faith is no longer 'Do you believe in God?', but 'Do you believe in your Ego, that it truly exists, that it transcends your ephemerality and darkness and is greater than you in your impotence and littleness?' "[1] Somehow we must come to believe that each one of us bears a part of human destiny within his true self, and each of us must do our utmost to bring this true self into being. We must also somehow come to realize that we will serve ourselves best by being loving and generous without expectation of return, for only in this way can we gain lasting contentment, happiness, and salvation. But how many are capable of this; how many have ever been capable of it?

Since every human act, even that of being oneself, has always been threatened with non-being, with nothingness, it has never been easy to be true to oneself. Few men have ever been capable of making the first step — that of accepting the fact of their death, of their meaninglessness, and of their guilt, of losing their

1. Vyacheslav Ivanov, *Freedom and the Tragic Life,* page 139.

life in order to find it — for in order to take this step, it is necessary to begin by recognizing oneself as a person. But such a recognition is extremely difficult today when man has become depersonalized and is the hapless victim of the tremendous impersonal forces which surround him. Faced with the inanities of starvation in the midst of plenty, of unemployment for millions when there was never a greater need or opportunity for productive work, of the tremendous waste of a cyclic economy of boom and bust; appalled by the horrors of wars which no one wants and which no one wins; dismayed by the ills of a decaying and degraded culture, of growing social evils, of spiritual poverty; beset by all these things, is it any wonder that modern man feels, as Sir Winston Churchill said in his Stockholm address, that "the fearful question confronts us: Have our problems got beyond our control?"

Modern man has arrived, at long last, at the end of a process of dehumanization. On all sides one still hears people prating of the sanctity of the individual, and even regards oneself as a person, but this is largely from force of habit. In the West, at any rate, the individual has lost his identity. For proof of this we need only consider that the two conflicting ideologies which are engaged in a struggle to the death for the possession of man's future, both regard him as an object.

If we compare the Marxian view of man with the traditional one subscribed to in the Western bourgeoise democracies, we are immediately struck by their apparent contradictions. But these contradictions are either on the surface, or they are illusory or insignificant. From the existentialist's point of view it is the similarities between Marxism and the Western bourgeoise attitudes toward man which are of far greater interest. We must never forget that Marx wrote his *Das Capital* in the British Museum during the reign of Queen Victoria, a period during which bourgeoise democracy and modern capitalism reached their ultimate development.

During this period, the accepted bourgeoise view of man was that if the individual was freed from legal restrictions, *laissez faire*, that he would naturally seek that which was to his best

20

interest; that is, the total result would be that economic, political, and social circumstances would be brought into greater accord with human reason and, as a consequence, man would be prosperous, happy, and content. It was believed, and still is for that matter, that "each man should strive to better himself at the cost of his neighbor, so as to coincide with the moral principle that all should labor for the common good."[1] So far as I know, Brooks Adams was the last man to recognize that there is a flat contradiction in this proposition.

Marx was deeply troubled by the anomalies which existed under this system — the great wealth of the few, and the great poverty of the many — but he did not repudiate its basic assumptions. Just as much as any Victorian economist, Marx regarded man as an object, a mere thing which is controlled and regulated by the economic, historical, political, and social circumstances which surround him. In his political and economic theories Marx proceeded largely on these assumptions; he believed that if these circumstances were altered and brought into greater accord with human reason and the needs of society, then man would be contented, prosperous, and happy. The great difference between the two ideas was in the means by which the ideal state was to be reached. In the place of the *laissez faire* of capitalism, Marx advocated political action, an intensification of the class struggle, revolution, and the establishment of a dictatorship of the proletariat. Fundamentally, however, Marx and the bourgeoisie of his day both subscribed to the view that the individual is equal to the sum of his social, political, and economic activities.

Today we stand as the heirs of the great Victorians whom we despise, but who built our world for us. And we have accepted their economic theories; not without question, of course, but we have accepted them. We tend to regard economic matters, as they did, in isolation from any moral, ethical, or humanitarian considerations. Our attitudes in such matters are reminiscent of

1. Henry Adams, *The Degradation of the Democratic Dogma*, Introduction by Brooks Adams, pages 78-79.

those utilitarians who piously denied themselves the luxury of rescuing the poor from misery for fear that they would be interfering with their liberties, or upsetting the delicate and mystical balance of the law of supply and demand — when *they* said *laissez faire*, they meant it. Our capitalistic economy is rarely defended upon moral or ethical grounds; indeed this would be extremely difficult as Brooks Adams pointed out. Even in its own efforts at apologetics, capitalism holds itself to be superior in that it produces more goods for more people than its rival. The inference is, of course, that increased production of goods is all that is ever needed to increase the sum of human happiness. The ironical part of this notion is that this same economy is never so sick, nor does it result in so much misery, as when it produces too much — but we will let that pass. The plain truth is this: we have come to regard ourselves, and one another, as a part of a process, as a necessary link in the chain of economic or political causation; as statistics; as producers or consumers; as employees or employers; as "the average man"; as "the buying public"; as occupants of some easily recognizable niche in the economic, social, and political scheme of things; and scarcely ever do we regard ourselves as individuals in the true sense, as unique, responsible persons whose every act, however insignificant, influences the outcome of world events. I sometimes wonder how much proof we need that such an attitude toward oneself and toward others is a dead-end for the human spirit.

It is only by becoming and remaining individuals, by being ourselves, that we can convert our anxieties into faith, into productive work, and into love. What we have learned to do instead, is to resort to violence in our attempts to overcome our anxieties of doubt and guilt. Because we cannot face the realization that every human act is meaningless and absurd (for all of our acts are meaningless except to the self we have destroyed); and because we cannot face the realization that there is no justification for faith, work, and love except in the value they add to the authentic individual existence which we have repudiated; because of these things, we torture one another — human suffering, we feel, certainly that has some meaning. And if we find it senseless, as we do, to build for a future which never comes, or to believe that despite our insignificance we have a full share in both the glory and the guilt of what man has wrought, still the conviction that destruction at least has meaning dies hard, and so we blunder on wreaking greater and greater destruction in the mistaken notion that we are somehow accomplishing something. As a result, our powers of destruction now far exceed our powers of building; and the fact that, so far, we construct more than we destroy, merely proves that man is an illogical and tragically confused creature who labors ceaselessly to create weapons which he dares not use even on his enemies. But because we haven't the courage to make the last and final step — to accept our absurdity and the courage of despair that rises from such an acceptance — because we regard our deaths with less distaste than we do the threat of non-being to all our acts; we humans will pull the pin on the final bomb before we will admit to ourselves that even torture, violence, and destruction are as superfluous, as gratuitous, and as meaningless as all the rest.

Regarded from this point of view, that part of modern art, music, and literature which I described earlier must come as a terrible warning. But it is our literature which most forcefully and undeniably voices this warning, for, of all the arts, literature is the most articulate. And our literature is the work of desperate men; men whose anguish and despair have driven them to see further and to see more clearly than it is possible for most of us to see. From my experience with the works of these men (and I often find myself an unwilling spectator, but sympathetic in the deepest sense), I am convinced that what they have seen has filled them with a sincere, deep, and genuine alarm for the future of man on this planet; hence their frenzied efforts to warn us before it is too late.

When we seek for examples of this warning in our literature, there is no need to confine ourselves to the work of authors of any particular country, for the confusion and alarm which transfigures much of modern writing is felt throughout the entire Western world and by people of all classes and of all ages. The

23

marijuana-smoking and desperately violent American adolescent, for example, has got the cruel barb of existence in his soul just as deep as those Pied Pipers of despair who crucify themselves on every page of their prose or in every line of their poetry, and both speak their eloquent warning.

It is the warning of Mr. T. S. Eliot's *Waste Land*: the picture of a waste of dead ideals, of dead souls, of dead cities and of the living dead who inhabit them, and of the dead gods who no longer watch over them. It is the warning of Conrad's *Typhoon,* a story in which we are shown a ship struggling in the enormous chaos of a brutal storm at sea, and the efforts of her crew to save her and themselves who will surely founder with her; a struggle which is carried out against the maniac forces of nature despite such distractions as the personal animosities and hatreds of the crew for one another, and a mob of Chinese coolies who are fighting like animals for some loose dollars which are rolling about in the hold. It is the warning that we must face on nearly every page of Faulkner's work: the warning that man is suffering and must continue to suffer a terrible retribution for the primordial sin of denial of freedom to himself and to others, his murder of God and of love, and his denial of self. For the Negro convict in the story which Faulkner calls *The Old Man,* the world is one of violence and terror, and he is adrift in the dark night, in the seething debris and destruction of a raging flood, where nameless and enormous objects strike at his skiff, and watersnakes slither out of the foam and over the gunwales. And how many others feel as he does, "cast upon a medium I was born to fear, to fetch up at last in a place I never saw before and where I do not even know where I am"? And are they not even inclined to feel, as he did, that escape is impossible, and that the security of a "monastic existence of shotguns and shackles" is preferable to freedom?[1]

It is the warning of W. H. Auden's *The Age of Anxiety,* that "many have perished; more will." As Van Wyck Brooks points

1. I am indebted here to Van Wyck Brooks, *The Writer in America.* Mr. Brooks has great gifts in selecting appropriate quotations.

out, the natural setting for Auden's poem, as for so many modern poems, plays, and stories, is the saloon, "where business looks up for the barman when necessity is associated with horror and freedom with boredom." Here there are always enough "lonelies," those who need what the barman has to give — "the sad haunters of Perhaps, who, estranged and aloof, brood over being till the bar closes."[1]

It is also the warning of the loveless world of Faulkner's *Wild Palms.*[2]

"Love if you will," says a Faulkner character, "because it can't last. There is no place for it in the world today. We have eliminated it. It took us a long time, but man is resourceful and limitless in inventing too, and so we have got rid of love at last, just as we have got rid of Christ. If Jesus returned today, we would have to crucify him quick in our own defense. If Venus returned, she would be a soiled man in a subway lavatory with a palm full of French post-cards."

But above all, it is the warning of James T. Farrell's great trilogy of futility and despair, *Studs Lonigan.* In his portrayal of the life and death of a young Irish-Catholic against the vast and hopeless setting of Chicago during the darkest years of the great American depression, Farrell has written one of the most terrible and frightening books that I have ever read. Studs, who is not without some fine qualities, seems to me to be a truly tragic figure in the modern sense. Throughout his entire life, which was nasty, brutish, and short, he does not do a single thing that could conceivably be regarded as having made the world a better place than he found it. His life is a constant and incessant repetition of his futility, frustration, stupidity, ignorance, and braggadocio; it is a life completely without meaning, without beauty, without joy, and even without animal satisfactions. The inexorable and terrifying lesson that Farrell forces upon us is that Studs was incapable of performing a single act which

1. Van Wyck Brooks, *The Writer in America,* page 118.
2. *Ibid.,* page 121, note.

was not a direct and inevitable result of his sordid environment. The result is that although we recognize him as an individual, we do so merely in the numerical or statistical sense, for we realize that the author could have employed any number of young men who lived in a large American city of the period to play the role; Studs Lonigan, we realize at last, never lived as a real person at all, not even in the novel which was devoted to him. For even his death was impersonal and fortuitous: he died of pneumonia after falling asleep in the snow on the way home from a drinking party. And on the night of his death, the most memorable thing that happened in the Lonigan household was that his father came home viciously drunk. Death in a dark room upstairs and drunken violence in the kitchen; so ended the existence of a pitiful object which was capable of motion and speech, but incapacitated for all that makes a real person — faith, work, and love.

Compared to Farrell's great symphony of futility, the trilogy of loneliness written by the Austrian Jew, Franz Kafka, is certainly much less unpleasant, less stark, and less alarming for most people. American authors, I believe, exhibit far more than they realize that indignation which comes from outraged ideals, particularly outrage at the corruption and degradation of the American dream. One of Faulkner's critics has pointed out, for example, that "outrage" is a key word in his work. As a nation we are still very young; and, like the very young, we find pessimism, cynicism, despair, and disillusionment foreign to our natures. I think it would do no harm to remind ourselves that when the young adopt cynical, pessimistic, and despairing attitudes, they are always a pose. I say this because there is certainly something of the pose, of affectation, in the violent writing of our novelists (who, by the way, are always young; there are no *old* American novelists still producing good work that I know of.) In Kafka, then, we miss, perhaps without regret, that peculiar combination of affected negativism and genuine outrage which is such a marked characteristic of much American writing. But Kafka's work has a haunting quality which may be, for some sensitive readers, even more deeply disturbing than the loud noises and violent coloring of writing by American hands. His perennial hero, K., has not even the distinction of a name, but his experiences are unforgettable.

In *America*, the first novel of the trilogy, the hero is twice disinherited and cast adrift in a world which is one vast concentration-camp, a world in which he encounters nothing but arbitrary power, false accusations, injustices, and maddening frustrations. He is lost in the interior of a ship, amid endless passages and flights of stairs, bereft of his possessions in the darkness; or he wanders blindly in a great fortress-like house with corridors that lead nowhere, blank walls, locked doors and empty rooms. A homeless wanderer in a world of sinister dwellings, and even more sinister men, who behave with as little rationality as people in a dream, he knows only persecution and frustration, with a sense of the utter futility of human effort.[1]

In *The Castle*, we see K. caught up in the ordeal of attempting to overcome his anxieties and to live a normal life. He arrives in a strange village which is dominated by a mysterious and enigmatic authority which is symbolized by the castle hidden in the mist above the town. Throughout the book (which, like *America*, has no proper ending), K. vainly attempts to obtain permission from the authorities in the castle to settle in the village and live a normal life. The novel is autobiographical, as all of Kafka's work is, and through the actions of K., Kafka expresses the solitude, the isolation of the artist and of the Jew who is an alien among the native born of life, the villagers who settle comfortably and naturally at the foot of the castle. But K. is denied what the villagers appear to have by natural right, and his actions reveal the inborn, self-distrustful solitariness which fights for order and regularity, for civic rights, for an established calling, for marriage; in short, for all the blisses of the commonplace. Through K., Kafka expresses his unbounded will, forever suffering shipwreck, to live aright: that is, to find God and win his approval, to perform productive work, and to love and be loved

1. Van Wyck Brooks, *The Writer in America*, page 125.

27

by another person. But in *The Castle*, when we last see K. he is still being denied these things.[1]

The Trial, however, opens with K. in a responsible and respectable position in society. Without warning he is visited one morning by a mysterious stranger who informs him of his arrest. K. is subsequently tried, condemned, and executed in the backlots of the town by two brutal assassins. Throughout his trial, which takes up nearly the whole of the novel, K. lives a life of dread, doubt, and perplexity. Despite his almost frantic efforts, he can discover neither the authority for his arrest, the identity of his accusers, the nature of the charges against him, or gain access to the judges who condemn him. The situation is baffling both to K. and to the reader, but it is not as unfamiliar to us in the United States as it once might have been.

It is impossible to convey the impression which this book leaves with you. It is a fantasy which is partly humorous, partly mad, yet incomparably sane and deadly serious; a fantasy in which the rather commonplace K. plays his baffling role against a backdrop of circumstance which is unsurpassed in literature for its muted terror. But the events of the story often strike one as playful, almost pleasant, and this, of course, is an effect with which all of us are familiar, for it is a constant element in animated cartoons. We have all smiled, many times, at the young and innocent animal who blunders comically into the waiting jaws of the cat, the wolf, or the crocodile. For those who have read it, as well as for those who may read it one day, I think it is important to remember that it is the work of a Jew. To a Jew, the hatred and condemnation of the anti-Semites by whom he is perpetually surrounded are as inexplicable as K.'s unknown crime and the unknown accusers and judges who condemn him and order his death. How many Jews who went to the gas-chambers of Dachau really understood why they were there; and who among us can answer *that* question?

But the novel is more than this, it is a full-length treatment of man's anxiety of guilt and condemnation. Even in his enjoy-

1. Franz Kafka, *The Castle*, homage by Thomas Mann.

ment of the blisses of the commonplace for which he yearned, K. stands guilty and condemned. This is an extreme view, but one which is familiar to those who are acquainted with the work of William Faulkner. One of Faulkner's characters says that in life you "walk the earth with your arm crooked over your head to dodge until you finally get the old blackjack at last and can lay back down again." And the old Indian chief in Faulkner's *The Old People* was called *Du Homme* ("Man"), until his tribesmen shortened his name to *Doom.*

Kafka's work, however, is unique in many ways. In his inimitable manner and with a brilliant style, he has, as Thomas Mann says, found salvation in writing of his despair, in accepting it and in shaping it into a work of art. He found, as Goethe had said, that "man can find no better retreat from the world than art, and man can find no stronger link with the world than art." Thomas Mann, who, in his own life, found the meaning of Goethe's saying, explains the nature of this art:[1]

> Art as the functioning of faculties bestowed by God, as work faithfully done; that is an interpretation not only in an intellectual but in a moral sense: as it heightens the actual into the true, it lends meaning and justification to life, not only subjectively but humanly; thus the work becomes humanly conservative, as a means of living "in the right" — or at least of coming closer to it — and art thus becomes adaptable to life.

These are the reflections of the great German novelist when writing of Kafka's tragic experience. I feel sure that he would agree with me when I say that if we wish to study the deadly and enervating perils that threaten human existence, we must read Kafka's novels; but if we wish to discover one possibility of overcoming them, we must study his life: denied faith and love, Kafka found some contentment, at last, in his art. But despite the temptation to dwell on this point it is time to go on to other matters.

1. Franz Kafka, *The Castle,* homage by Thomas Mann.

I have been hitting about rather haphazardly in my selections of recent authors who bear evidence to my contention that our literature, as well as our other arts, stands as a warning which we disregard at our utmost peril. This lack of system, however, is probably due to the nature of the literature which has been produced in the past fifty or so years, a period during which the tendencies which I have been describing have been international rather than national. This literature, of course, as I have already mentioned, is not all of one suit, no need to pretend that it is, but it is rather like a pinochle deck: if you turn up a card you may not find the ace of spades or the black queen, but you stand a pretty good chance of turning up one of her sisters, a knave, or a joker.

It is interesting to observe that the first full-length portrait of man drawn from the existentialistic point of view appeared nearly a century ago in the heyday of Queen Victoria's reign, when all the world was young, and all the grass was green (or so we suppose). The author of this piece was Henrik Ibsen, the Norwegian poet and playwright, whose existentialistic play, *Peer Gynt,* appeared in 1867. At that time, Soren Kierkegaard, the founder of the existentialistic movement, had already been dead for over thirty years, but inasmuch as he had written all of his books in Danish, a language unfamiliar to most Europeans, he was not known outside his own country except in Norway where Danish was the official court language. This is one reason why Kierkegaard's work remained almost unknown in Europe and America until fifty or so years ago when it was first translated into German.

It is well known that Ibsen was a great admirer of the work of Kierkegaard; but even if we were ignorant of this fact, the marks of the Danish existentialist's influence are too strong in Ibsen's work to leave any question in our minds. Ibsen's lyric drama, *Peer Gynt,* is a satiric-fantasy of the Norwegian character and a tragedy of a lost soul. If one views it narrowly, it can also be read as an existentialistic tract. Of course it is a great deal more than that, for it is the work of a great artist and also one of the best things he ever did. For this reason I earnestly hope that my mauling it about in this clumsy fashion will not spoil it for anyone; but, at the same time, I intend to pursue my point of view, as narrow as it admittedly is, in the belief that an understanding of the central problem presented in the play will prove as interesting as some of its more charming, if less vital, aspects.

Ibsen's Peer Gynt is a personable but worthless young fellow who has a glib tongue, a way with girls, and a great deal of cheek. It is fitting, therefore, that his career should be an infinite variety of ups and downs. Starting as a penniless peasant boy, he ventures forth into the world to become a slave-trader in America; then a merchant of heathen idols, rum, and Bibles in the Orient; then he loses everything and becomes a pauper; then he recoups by setting up as a prophet in the Arabian desert; again a pauper; and, at last, aged and world-weary, returns home. In all things Peer adheres to his motto, "unto thyself be enough"; and in all things he is concerned about nothing quite so much as that there should always be an easy way out. He is, therefore, the very incarnation of an uncompromising dread of decisive committal to any one course. Hence his perpetual "hedging" and his determination never to engage himself in anything to the extent that he cannot easily draw back. Hence his fragmentary life of smatterings. Hence his deep-rooted selfishness and cynical indifference to all higher motives. And hence, above all, his sordid and superstitious religion, for to him religion is the apotheosis of the art of hedging.

On his return home, Peer meets a comical little fellow who carries a button molder's ladle in which he melts all the human souls which are not worth keeping. Peer is horrified to learn that inasmuch as he is neither evil enough for hell, nor good enough for heaven, he is to go into the ladle with the rest. He complains bitterly to the Button Molder who finally tells him, by way of explanation why he is to go into the ladle, that the simple truth is he has never been himself. Peer is incredulous: he has never been anything but himself, that has been his trouble all along. The Button Molder, however, reminds Peer that what he says is not strictly true: instead of being true to

31

himself, he has merely been sufficient unto himself, which is not the same thing at all. Peer is sobered, but by no means convinced:

> Peer. One question — just one: what is it, at bottom, this "being oneself?"
> Button Molder. To be oneself is to slay oneself.
> But on you the answer is doubtless lost;
> And therefore we'll say: to stand forth everywhere
> With Master's intention displayed like a sign-board.
> Peer. But suppose a man never has come to know what Master meant with him?
> Button Molder. He must divine it.
> Peer. But how oft are divinings beside the mark;
> Then one's sometimes carried off in mid-career
> Before one reaches his full development.
> Button Molder. That is certain, Peer Gynt: in default of divining the cloven-hoofed gentleman finds his best hook.
> Peer. This matter is excessively complicated. . . .[1]

It is true, as Peer complains, the matter *is* excessively complicated; but perhaps I can assist the Button Molder by commenting and enlarging upon this passage, and by reminding Peer of the lesson of his own experience.

As the Button Molder observed, God meant something when he made each one of us. To be oneself is to embody that meaning in one's words and deeds. But in order to be himself, a man must slay himself. That is, he must slay the craving to make himself the center round which all others revolve. But what if a person fails to figure out what God did mean him to be? Why then he must *feel* it. Perhaps it is just here that our education fails us, for the way most of us are educated tends to enhance our intellects at the expense of our emotions; as a result, when our intellects fail us we have no other resource.

1. Ibsen, *Peer Gynt,* trans. William Archer, page 252 f.

Few of us realize, I believe, how insufficient the intellect is when we attempt to discover our true selves.

It is easy, as everyone knows, to find a refuge from facts in lies, in self-deception, and in self-sufficiency. It is easy, for example, to take credit for what circumstances have done for us, and to blame circumstances for what we owe to ourselves. It is easy to think that we are realizing ourselves by refusing to become a "pack-horse for the troubles of others," keeping alternatives open and never closing a door behind us and so remaining the master of the situation and self-possessed. But if we choose to do these things, as Peer Gynt did, we may always "get round" our difficulties, but we will never get through them. It is true we will always remain master of the situation, but the situations will become poorer and narrower every day. The point is — and it is one that Jean-Paul Sartre is never tired of making — that if we never commit ourselves, we never express our true self, and our self becomes less and less significant and decisive. Calculating selfishness is the annihilation of self, for when we have denied or destroyed the self which God gave us, we go into the ladle to be melted down with all the other dross and damaged human goods.[1]

But in order to live a dedicated life, as Sartre and the Button Molder exhort us to do, we must live a life of faith, of love, and of productive work. And this has certainly never been easy, nor is it easy today in a world in which, as Nietzsche said, God is dead — as indeed he is for many people. Nor has it ever been easy to love. "It's quite a job starting to love somebody," says one of Sartre's characters. "You have to have energy, generosity, blindness. There is even a moment, in the very beginning, when you have to jump across a precipice: if you think about it you don't do it." And, of course, we have already had the rather discouraging news from Faulkner that in our world love is dead too. And if we are denied faith and love, how is it possible to work productively and creatively as God has intended that we should? We cannot all follow the example of Franz Kafka, who

1. Ibsen, *Peer Gynt,* William Archer's introduction.

produced memorable literature though it cost him a cry of anguish for every word. What, then, are we to do?

This is a problem which has occupied many of our best writers, and one which they have announced in their frantic warnings to us. It is a problem for which many of them have found at least a partial answer which has been formalized in the philosophy of existentialism. In the next section I want to examine some of their answers, and also to have a look at that rather enigmatic philosophy.

EXISTENTIALISM AND MODERN LITERATURE

Up to this point, I have dwelt on my theme in a rather discursive manner. Now, however, it is time to consolidate some of the diverse matter which I have brought before the reader. First of all, I would like to attempt to answer the question, what is an existentialist? But before I begin, perhaps I should warn the reader, as well as myself, that we must be very cautious in our use of this term. For one thing, it cannot be said, except in a very general way, that there is a philosophy of existentialism; there are only existentialistic thinkers. And this is a reflection of the fact that nowhere does there exist a comprehensive system of thought which can be called the philosophy of existentialism.

H. J. Blackham's *Six Existentialistic Thinkers* bears out this contention; his survey of the work of Kierkegaard, Nietzsche, Heidegger, Jaspers, Sartre, and Marcel covers a great deal of ground in time, space, and ideas. Kierkegaard, a Dane, is probably best described as a primitive Christian and mystic; an outstanding characteristic of his thought is its revolt from the extreme rationalism of Hegel. It would take a brave man to attempt to classify Frederich Nietzsche, a German, whose frenzied utterances can scarcely be regarded as the product of any recognizable rational process, but result from the sort of apocalyptic intuitions that moved the more ecstatic Hebrew prophets. Heidegger, a former professor of philosophy in a German university, has probably inspired more existentialistic writing than he has committed (Sartre and Jaspers both owe him a great deal), but I am not so certain that his own work has not been largely misinterpreted — in any event, he has apparently reached a position now which his earlier admirers find very baffling. Jaspers, another German, is also a professor of philosophy — a coincidence which has brought about the rather ribald observation that existentialism is only an occupational disease of men in his position. He was a student of Heidegger's, but one who went his own way and is currently occupying a position very similar to that of the Frenchman, Gabriel Marcel, whose existentialistic speculations have led him to embrace the Catholic faith. Nor is the example of both Jaspers and Marcel to be wondered at, for the existentialistic characteristics of Christian thought, as exemplified in the writings of such men as St. Paul, St. Augustine, and St. Thomas Aquinas, are greatly admired by many serious existentialists.

Some indication of the diversity of the group, however, is indicated by the presence of Jean-Paul Sartre, an atheistic existentialist who, though he begins by postulating the nonexistence of God, reaches and sustains a very high and challenging level of morality and ethics in his social writings. (The level of morality in his novels is another matter. But I do not think we should be misled by the absurdly naive belief that he dwells on the sordid because he is infatuated by it. On the contrary, the title of his first novel, and the one that is generally regarded as his best, is *Nausea.*)

This should serve to remind us, I think, that the existentialists do not represent a defection from the Christian tradition (i.e. they are not a new sect of Protestants), but are a group of thinkers who are attempting to develop an alternative religious discipline as a guide for living in the chaos of the modern world. On the other hand, to say that they have set themselves up in competition to the Christian faith is going much too far. Kierkegaard, for example, said of himself that all his life he had been trying to become a Christian. It seems to me, therefore, that most of their best efforts have been devoted to reviving the kind of religious faith which is dead for many people in the modern world. The conversion of Gabriel Marcel is interesting from this point of view, for Marcel moved from agnosticism through existentialism to Catholicism, and is now regarded as an outstanding Christian existentialist.

As I have already stated, none of the men I have mentioned has attempted to establish a system, nor have they given any indication of a desire to do so. They seem to be fully aware of the criticism that their thinking lacks method and even plain logic. To such criticism they have replied: We have had enough of systems; we are not interested in metaphysics, we are interested in man and the problems of his existence. And their preoccupation with these problems, of course, is a reflection of the perilous situation in which we find ourselves. "Make no mistake," says Oswald Spengler, who is something of an existentialist himself, "what we are experiencing is no mere crisis in the affairs of the West, it is the beginning of a catastrophe." There is certainly some similarity between the relationship of existentialism to the present situation, and the relationship of early Christianity to the break-up of the Roman Empire. The question: What must we do to be saved? is being asked by more and more men, and it is being asked with a fervency unknown to the West since the Renaissance.

The answer given by the existentialists to this question is threefold:

1. first we must find out how to live.
2. but in order to do this, we must find out who we are and what kind of person each of us was meant to be.
3. there is also implied in this search for the true nature of the self, the implication of choice; and the most significant choice that a man can make is his choice of death, for nothing reveals the true nature of a man as the manner of his dying — witness Socrates and Christ.

But we have all heard this before, and what has it ever come to? Well, I admit that it does sound a little simple-minded. But so do some of the most profound religious truths that have sustained men in the past — the notion of Divine Providence is the first example which comes to mind. The difficulty, it seems to me, lies not so much in finding the truth — which "cries out in the streets, though no man heeds it," as Shakespeare says — as it lies in acting upon it. Which means that it is not sufficient for us to know the truth, we must become the truth; we must become, in other words, living examples of what the truth means to us. And in order to do this, we must become the person we

37

were intended to be, and we must also fulfill our obligation as men to leave the world a better place than we have found it.

But once again this is probably all too obvious.

Still, while I freely admit to the charge of belaboring what all men already know, I cannot help but wonder how many really understand what they appear to know so well. Could any man, knowing the simple truths which I have just mentioned, willfully commit an act which would make the world a worse place to live in? I am not speaking of those who are misguided by their faith, whatever it is; nor do I mean the unenlightened, the ignorant who do evil mistaking it for good. No, the ones who concern me are those of us who know that what they are doing is wrong, but who do it all the same. For every criminal and unjust act which is inspired by personal greed, ambition, lust for power, or hatred, is a deliberate blow at the fabric of our civilization which, in Nietzsche's words, is already "sick unto death."

But let us be reasonable: would any rational person undermine the foundations of the structure upon which his survival depends? Well, hardly! And yet we know that this goes on every day. Have men suddenly become irrational? I do not think that this is the answer, and if I may be permitted to take the reader aside for a moment, I would like to ask him a question which I believe will point to the solution. Do you, as an individual, believe that by your ordinary actions, you have a determining influence on the course of worldly events? Do you believe that by your own actions you can overcome the evils of Communism, the threat of atomic warfare, and keep the "catastrophe" which Spengler has foreseen from visiting our Western world? If you do, I would like to congratulate you for your uncommon perception and moral fortitude, for I assure you in what you must already know, that such an attitude is far from common.

The truth is, of course, that most of us are persuaded that our individual actions are all but meaningless, and we tend to regard ourselves as the victims of wars, depressions, and national and world calamities of all descriptions, rather than as the authors of them. We are the victims, the hapless objects which are caught up and carried along by forces over which we have no control.

The person who knowingly performs a crime against society, any anti-social act, has convinced himself that his actions have no influence on the outcome of human events or he wouldn't be so foolish. This observation brings us to a fourth point which is common to nearly all existentialistic thinkers: that is, their profound conviction that not only do our individual actions determine the outcome of worldly events, but that we are personally and individually responsible for the condition of the world in which we are living. In other words, these men insist that if I see and recognize the evil about me, and do nothing about it, then I have chosen evil — it is as simple as that.

But this brings up the question of whether the world we find ourselves in is such an evil one. Opinions regarding this matter, as in everything else that ever was or ever will be, differ. But there is a surprising, not to say frightening, unanimity of opinion among sober men today that our condition could stand nothing so much as improvement. One of the most notorious portraits of our world, as well as of ourselves who live in it, was drawn a generation ago by T. S. Eliot in a poem which he appropriately entitled *The Waste Land*. This rather depressing piece was successful enough to give its name to the period between the two wars.

The world, as seen by Mr. Eliot, is the dreary spiritual desert of modern London, a city which he portrays as the decayed and enervated refuse of a civilization gone stale. (Actually it seems he rather overstated his case: the Londoners of the blitz, including Mr. Eliot himself, showed a surprising amount of vitality — but every truth must be overstated to cover up the falsehood that is always mixed with it.)

Mr. Eliot's Waste Land is populated by the Hollow Men whom he has celebrated in another short poem:

> We are the hollow men
> We are the stuffed men
> Leaning together
> Headpiece filled with straw. Alas!
> Our dried voices, when
> We whisper together

Are quiet and meaningless
As wind in dry grass
Or rat's feet over broken glass
In our dry cellar.

Shape without form, shade without color,
Paralyzed force, gesture without motion;

Those who have crossed
With direct eyes, to death's other kingdom
Remember us — if at all — not as lost
Violent souls, but only
The stuffed men.

One cannot help but be reminded by this of Dante's "Trimmers," the vast majority of the dead who reside in the ante-room of hell — those

> . . . who lived without blame, and without praise . . . but were for themselves. . . . Those who have no hope of death because they were never really alive: and whose blind life is so mean, that they are envious of every other lot, those who could not even enter hell because the damned would have some glory over them.

Such are the inhabitants of Eliot's spiritual desert of *The Waste Land,* the hollow men, the stuffed men filled with straw. Such people as these are not really alive because their existence is merely a conditioned reflex, an automatic gesture, a nervous twitch over which they have no control.

But no one, the existentialists tell us, can exist authentically unless he meets his obligation to make a choice, to exercise his free will. A tiger, they say, can exist authentically by being just like any other tiger. But each of us is given his existence with only a potential essence — for each of us has in him the substance of some unique divine intention. Robert Browning recognizes this incompleteness in man in his poem *A Death in the Desert,* where he contrasts man with God and animals:

> "God is," says Browning, "they are, man partly is and wholly hopes to be."

In short, Browning recognizes that no man can live authentically as a man until he decides what kind of a person he is meant to be, and then becomes that kind of person. Which means, of course, that a man has to choose his own destiny, for in deciding what kind of a person he is to become, he also decides his fate. Heraclitus, the pre-Socratic Greek philosopher, knew this very well when he said that "a man's character is his destiny."

But all that I have just said, of course, is contingent upon the assumption that man has a capacity to choose — that is, that he has free will. And this question of free will, at least in the West, is one which has given rise to a great deal of rather fruitless controversy in the past, and appears likely to give rise to an ever-increasing amount of discussion in the future. While I cannot hope to settle this problem once and for all, after so many wiser men have failed, still I would like to throw whatever light upon it I can. It is much to the credit of the existentialists, I believe, that they have finally reduced the discussion to absurdity. To take only one example, Sartre's insistence that man is not only "condemned to be free," but that he "*is* his freedom," may not satisfy everyone, but it certainly puts things in a different light.

The psychological determinists among us will argue until doomsday that man's free will is an illusion. Let us grant it to them—for many men it is. But, as Dante tells us, those who choose neither good nor evil cannot properly be called men at all, they are merely the "Trimmers" of life, and the tragic thing is that they outnumber all the rest, as they do in Dante's Inferno. If our determinist friends want to join these Hollow Men, let them — they will have the comfort of knowing that they are travelling with the majority. But as for those who do not follow the crowd, let us warn them that they have no choice but to choose — they are, in Sartre's memorable words, "condemned to be free." In other words, no man can live authentically, say the existentialists, until he begins to exercise his power of choice — "a man," says Karl Jaspers, "is the sum of his choices."

If there was ever any doubt in my mind as to the validity of the existentialist's insistence upon the necessity of choice, it was dispelled as soon as I saw clearly that it was essentially the same message as that brought to the West by Socrates and Christ. In

41

choosing a cruel death, rather than an ignominious life, both of these great teachers revealed an advanced stage of human existence toward which the rest of mankind could hopefully aspire, for both men had divine missions which they would not repudiate. And their divine mission was made manifest by their refusal to negate their own individuality: faced with torture and death, they held firm to their choices of truth and love.

The ethical implications of the example of Socrates are inescapable. He could not obey the law — that is, he would not promise to keep his mouth shut, which was all that was asked of him — because he believed the law to be unjust in that it attempted to conceal the truth which God had chosen him to seek out. At the same time, however, he felt that he could not attempt to escape his punishment without repudiating his previous choice of remaining in Athens and raising his family under its laws. The cup of hemlock was inevitable, for it was the one authentic choice which he could make and thereby set the seal of authenticity on all that had gone before. If he had not drunk the hemlock, he would not have been Socrates. That is the divine paradox: in freely choosing to give up his life, he immortalized himself; in Christian terms, he found his life in losing it.

But it is to Christ that we in the West must look for the supreme example of an authentic existence, for in the symbolism of his Trial, Passion, and Resurrection, we can read of the glorious consummation of a divinely inspired human existence. In its essence, the choice that Christ made was the same as that of Socrates; only it was a higher choice in that he made it on the basis of love, not truth. (Among all the accusers of Socrates, I am certain that it never occurred to one of them that he was guilty of loving his fellow men.) Like the choice of Socrates, the choice that Christ made was an inevitable one; inevitable, that is, because he was who and what he was. I do not mean to suggest that he had to make this choice, any more than the old man Socrates had to make his. What I am striving to convey here is the idea, which I see so clearly, that it was in making the choice of his painful death that Christ revealed his divine mission, that he was "the Son of God." But without thus choosing himself, he could not have done this; for if he had escaped his torture and death, and he could have easily done so time after time, would he have been the same? Without that choice which shook the world, would we admit his "divinity;" would we even attempt, in our feeble way, to follow his example if it had not, in the end, led to that fatal tree? And did he or did he not prove for all time that a simple choice can move the world?

After having said so much, I am aware that there are many who must find much to object to in all this. By putting Christ and Socrates on the same level, they will say, you demean our Saviour. This is pious, but inaccurate; and I suspect that Socrates himself might find it a little offensive. For myself, I would not attempt to judge between the two, though I certainly feel the impact of Christ's example far more acutely than that of Socrates — though this was not always so with me. But I really feel that we have no basic quarrel. I have rendered the Christian message in my own words simply because I too must understand what I am saying, and I find that the traditional terminology fails to express the partial insight I have had into the truth that is Christ. The reader may not agree with either my method or my motives, and he may be absolutely right in rejecting both. But it is interesting, I think, that men of such divergent minds and talents as T. S. Eliot, William Faulkner, and Arthur Miller seem to be remarkably intent on propagating this same idea.

Mr. Faulkner, for example, in an elaborate re-working of the Passion which he calls *The Fable,* has one of his characters make the following observations on the coming execution of the corporal who is the Christ-figure in the allegory:

"If he accepts his life, he will have abrogated his own gesture and martyrdom. If I gave him his life tonight, I myself could render null and void what you call the hope and the dream of his sacrifice. By destroying his life tomorrow morning, I will establish forever that he didn't even live in vain, let alone die so."

This is the father of the corporal speaking; in other words, the character who stands for God the Father in the allegory. But for those who are familiar with Faulkner's work, this will come as no surprise, for Faulkner has never denied the importance of this kind of choice.

Mr. Eliot, on the other hand, has been a long while arriving at the same conclusion, and he has done so in seeming contradiction to much that he has said before; but there is no need to quarrel with him about that, nor should we look a gift prophet in the mouth. His two plays, *The Cocktail Party* and *The Confidential Clerk,* for example, contain much that is interesting from the point of view which I have been developing. And, incidentally, they also contain a great deal that is disappointing to his disciples; but this is not the first time that this has happened. It sometimes seems to me that Mr. Eliot has left more broken hearts behind him than any poet since Byron. It would be a curious study to attempt to discover why he so persistently disappoints the best hopes and expectations of his followers. I do not pretend to have the answer, but I can offer one clue that might possibly turn out to be helpful.

The two plays which I am going to consider briefly should have been written, I believe, in reverse order. In other words, it seems to me that *The Confidential Clerk,* his latest product, should have appeared before *The Cocktail Party,* which was first produced in 1949. Many things seem to point to this: the earlier play is on a major theme, the later on a minor one; it is more mature, and has greater depth; and, for our purposes, trivial as they may be, the plays would make a great deal more sense if they had appeared in the order in which I intend to deal with them. Perhaps the cause of all the misunderstanding between Mr. Eliot and his admirers is that he is approaching the problem of man's existence from a direction which no one has suspected possible — and, of course, this is always the prerogative of a man of genius, besides being Mr. Eliot's way. I offer the suggestion for what it is worth.

But let us turn to the plays. As I have stated, it is my intention to take them up in reverse order, as they seem to me to make more sense that way.

In *The Confidential Clerk,* we have Mr. Eliot's treatment of the interesting problem of establishing the identity of the self. The confidential clerk, the protagonist, is Colby Simpkins, who is preoccupied throughout the work with the question Who am I? and What kind of a person am I supposed to be?

At the beginning of the piece, young Colby thinks he knows the answers to both these questions, and he is ordering his life accordingly. He knows who he is: the illegitimate son of Sir Claude Mulhammer, a very successful financier, for whom he is acting as a private secretary, or confidential clerk. Colby has taken this position because he is convinced that his failure as a musician — he aspired to play the organ but gave up in despair when he discovered that he had no talent for it — has made it plain that he must seek some other career for himself. And he is reassured in his decision when he learns that his father, Sir Claude, was also a disappointed artist of sorts. Sir Claude tells him that he wanted to be a potter, not a financier, but that his own father had persuaded him that his best hopes for success in life lay in the other direction — and he adds that he is now convinced that his father was right. When Colby tells him that "the other person" whom he feels himself becoming, and whom he sometimes fears and dislikes, is accused by the disappointed organist in him, Sir Claude tells him:

". . . I loathed this occupation
Until I began to feel my power in it.
The life changed me, as it is changing you:
It begins as a kind of make-believe
And the make-believing makes it real."

Sir Claude continues:

"But that's not the whole story. My father knew I hated it.
That was a grief to him. He knew, I am sure,
That I cherished for a long time a secret reproach;
But after his death, and then it was too late,
I knew that he was right. And all my life
I have been atoning. To a dead father,
Who had always been right. I never understood him.
I was too young. And when I was mature enough
To understand him, he was not there."

Now this is a very moving appeal for a father to make to his son, and I am certain that we can all sympathize with Colby for

45

inclining toward his father's wishes. But as for the proposal itself, nothing could be more vicious and calculated to cause mortal mischief than this fatherly advice however well-intended it may have been. And Colby himself recognizes this as soon as it becomes plain that Sir Claude is not his father at all, but a stranger.

The reason for Colby's uneasiness when he feels that he is being accused by the ghost of his true self, the disappointed musician, is that he is forced to realize that he is not living an authentic existence — in other words that he is really, and not merely conventionally, illegitimate. What Sir Claude is advising him to do is to slay the ghost of his true self and thus set himself free to become someone else, a different kind of person than he was intended to be. But such an action, as Sir Claude unwittingly makes clear, is a sin against oneself, even though it appears to be dutiful to a parent. I strongly suspect that Sir Claude's own feeling of guilt is not caused by his inward disobedience to his own father's wishes, but by his outward obedience in following his advice (the same advice he is now giving Colby), to murder his true self; and the source of this guilt is his sin against himself. As a matter of fact, every sin we commit is of this nature: that is, the denial and abrogation of self; the thwarting of our destiny; the deliberate choice of an inauthentic existence; the turning of our backs on the good that is in us.

It is left to one of the other characters, however, to point out the source of our obligation to choose and to live an authentic existence, and to be the person we were intended to become:

". . . there's something in us," says Lady Elizabeth,
"In all of us, which isn't just heredity,
But something unique. Something we have been
From eternity. Something straight from God.
That means that we are nearer to God than to anyone."

But Sir Claude obviously wants Colby to be closer to him than to anyone else, God included, and therefore he advises him to put aside the unique person that God intended him to be. It must be plain to everyone, however, that Colby cannot do this without doing violence to God's will: without, that is, sinning against the divine principle within him. The situation seems plain enough:

because he loves the man whom he believes to be his son, and because he wants him close to him, Sir Claude becomes the devil's advocate. And Colby, because he loves the man he believes to be his father, takes — but for a time only — the course which must surely damn him. Is it any wonder, then, that Christ gives us the advice that we must forsake even our parents if we wish to be saved?

The plot of this play is almost unbelievably complex, and Mr. Eliot's ingenuity in springing surprise after surprise of recognition on his audience would have delighted the Restoration dramatists; and, I believe, the play would have delighted Aristotle himself, who rather favored this sort of thing. It seems to me that the play is little more than an elaborate revival of that old-faithful of 19th century drama and fiction, the long-lost child returned to his rightful inheritance, and its appeal is not very different. But it is not my purpose to classify nor to attempt to unravel the tangled skein of relationships with which Mr. Eliot snares his reader.

The important thing is that Colby, after he finds that he is not the illegitimate son of Sir Claude, nor the long-lost son of Lady Elizabeth, nor the half-brother of Lucasta, nor any relation whatsoever to Barnabas Kaghan; but that he is, after all, the son of a second-rate organist, he finally decides that he is meant to be just that. In short, when he discovers that his real father was also an unsuccessful musician, like himself, he declares his intention of returning to the music for which he has no real talent. Having at last found out who he is and what kind of a man he was intended to be, Colby rejects his inauthentic existence as Sir Claude's natural son and secretary, and announces his legitimacy:

> "As long as I believed that you were my father
> I was content to have had the same ambitions
> And in the same way to accept their failure.
> But now I want to be an organist
> It doesn't matter about success."

Of course there is a great deal more to the play than this. Like everyone else in it, during the three acts Sir Claude learns much that he did not know about himself, and this self-knowledge enables him to have a much greater understanding of the others, particularly his wife with whom he had apparently been living for twenty years as a complete stranger. He realizes, for example, that his self-sacrifice was not enough:

"I might have been truer to my father's inspiration," he tells his wife, "if I had done what I wanted to do."

And he finds, to his great surprise, that his aristocratic and fashionable wife would have respected him for it. But this is merely one more example of Mr. Eliot's constant use of the device of surprise recognitions to bring his characters to self knowledge.

It was the ancient Greeks, with whom Mr. Eliot is well acquainted, who were the first to recognize that all knowledge begins with this knowledge of the self. But I believe that it is only the existentialists at the present time who have gone as far as Mr. Eliot has in this play in stressing the subjectivity of all knowledge. Both he and they are convinced that unless you follow the admonition at Delphi, which was also Socrates' motto, "Know Thyself," that you will never know anything at all. And both they and he, though I am not so certain that Mr. Eliot would be specially pleased to be included in such curious company, go even further than this. The existentialists, for example, insist that it is not sufficient to know the truth, we must become the truth. In other words, they insist that we must become a living example of what we know to be true.

But if my knowledge of what is true depends upon my knowledge of the true nature of my self, then what is true for me may not be true for anyone else: as a matter of fact, what is true for me is only true for me and cannot be true for anyone else.

Exactly!

The truth was that it was better for Colby to be a second-rate musician than it was for him to be a first-rate secretary. *But this was true only for Colby!* And he could not, nor did he, recognize the truth of this for him until he had actually committed himself irrevocably to the career of a mediocre musician. It was only after he had actually become a second-rate musician that either he or anyone else could realize that he had made an authentic existential choice.

Sir Claude, on the other hand, could not recognize until too late that it might have been better for him to have been a second-rate potter than a highly successful financier. His choice, though it brought him great rewards, was obviously inauthentic; but we shall never know what would have been best for him because until such a choice is actually made, one cannot determine its authenticity.

The example of Sir Claude should make it clear that Mr. Eliot believes that often more is lost in success than in failure. The practising psychiatrist, as Erich Fromm points out, frequently has good reason to be uneasy when he realizes that the well-adjusted individual may be less of a person than the neurotic whom he is attempting to "adjust." If the world is mad, as it frequently appears to be, then perhaps it is better to be "out of joint," like Hamlet, than well-suited to the times like Polonius. If this sounds paradoxical, I might mention that our own behavior in regards to the unusual individual is also rather perplexing. Is it not true that while we honor and revere genius, at the same time we often appear to be doing our best, or our worst, to stamp it out? Does not the struggle for recognition which genius undergoes suggest that we place some penalty on it? And if the genius must struggle painfully to become that person which God intended him to be, think how much more difficult it is for the ordinary person who does not have genius to sustain him — Colby Simpkins could certainly tell us about this. And yet this struggle for self-hood, or for the recognition of individuality, must be carried on by each of us until death interrupts our efforts.

For this reason, the existentialists, as well as Mr. Eliot, maintain that it is not sufficient to hold the truth, nor to become a living example of the truth we hold, we must also be prepared to die for the truth which we have become — for this is the one sure proof of an authentic existence. I will not deny that this sounds a bit drastic, but it is exactly the principle which forms the theme of Mr. Eliot's very fashionable play, *The Cocktail Party.*

In this play we are once again confronted with an exceedingly complex plot — one might almost say tedious. At first glance the play appears to be a somewhat overdrawn portrait of a trivial and superficial society that is talking itself to death. But I suspect that Mr. Eliot chose this means of conveying to us his little seed of wisdom, since we are interested in nothing quite so much as our own portraits. It is by showing us our triviality and futility that Mr. Eliot can make his rather stern and rigorous solution to the problem of man's existence appear believable.

There is also a great deal of mumbo-jumbo in the play, but it cannot conceal the "message" — and that message is the one which flamed on Calvary, that he who loses his life shall find it. To the sceptical reader who is prepared to be surprised at the appearance of the crucifixion symbol in such a setting, I would like to point out that Mr. Eliot is faithful not only to the topographical details of the Passion, but he even echoes the language of that fateful hour. When his priest-psychiatrist sets the seal of his blessing on the one authentic existence which appears in the play — that of the adulterous Miss Celia Coplestone — he borrows from St. John:

"It is finished," he says, as he dismisses her to her doom.

As the play opens, we find that Edward and Lavinia Chamberlayne are giving a cocktail party. It soon appears, however, that the hostess, in the press of the more urgent business of leaving her husband, has forgotten all about the affair. As a consequence, her husband is doing his noble best to entertain the few guests he had failed to reach in his efforts to call the whole thing off. Under very trying circumstances Edward manages somehow to keep things going. And it is in this first scene that we see him at his best, for he shows more courage and character in facing his unwanted and prying guests than he does at any point in the play.

This is enough, I believe, to give us some idea of the quality of this "well-matched" couple, and of their play. For it is their play: all of the action evolves from them and their cocktail party which keeps reappearing as the action progresses. (As it finally turns out, we learn that their destiny is to face the complete futility and emptiness of their loveless lives, but to go bravely on giving party after party, and, at the final curtain, they are waiting for another to begin.)

50

Of course others are involved. Celia Coplestone, whom I have already mentioned, interests us for two reasons: one is that she is Edward's mistress; and the other, that she is the only real person in the play (a point which I shall come back to presently.)

The others can be dismissed briefly. Peter Quilpe, a young admirer of Miss Coplestone's, spends most of his time in Hollywood (the scene of the play is London), and his part in the play is functional rather than significant. Alexander MaColgie Gibbs and Julia Shuttlethwaite are so thoroughly involved in the mumbo-jumbo that I do not pretend to understand them, nor even to believe in them if I did.

This leaves us only Sir Henry Harcourt-Reilly, a psychiatrist, who pushes the levers which move the dramatic machinery. Sir Henry, I suggest, is rather naively drawn: he is a curious composition of the psychoanalyst and the priest, and he performs something of the functions of both. I recall that Paul Tillich once wrote that a good psychiatrist would also have to be something of a father confessor to his patients — perhaps this is what Mr. Eliot had in mind when he drew Sir Henry.

As it is fairly obvious that none of these people are worth a second thought, the reader has a right to be curious as to my reasons for selecting this play for examination here. The answer to both our doubts as to the validity of the choice lies in the person of Miss Celia Coplestone.

As I have already mentioned, Celia is involved with Edward Chamberlayne in an extra-marital love affair. When Edward's wife leaves him, there is an inevitable crisis in the relationship between himself and Celia. Both are rather stunned to discover that they have been fooling themselves, as well as each other, for a long time; and this realization forces them face to face with their true selves which each had been attempting to escape by using the other. Edward is the first to realize this:

"I see that my life was determined long ago
And that the struggle to escape from it
Is only a make-believe, a pretence
That what is, is not, or could be changed.
The self that can say 'I want this — or want that' —

The self that wills — he is a feeble creature;
He has to come to terms in the end
With the obstinate, the tougher self; who does not speak,
Who never talks, who cannot argue;
And who in some men may be the *guardian* —
But in men like me, is the dull, the implacable,
The indomitable spirit of mediocrity."

From this point on, Edward's role, which takes up a great deal of the rest of the play, is that of a man who is trying to learn to live with the truth about himself; that is, to reconcile himself to his mediocrity, his futility, and his incapacity to love anyone — not even himself.

But Celia's true self is something quite different. When she pays a professional visit to Sir Henry's consulting room — as all the leading characters do — he offers her a choice of two cures for her feeling of guilt, the guilt of living inauthentically. One cure would be reconciliation to an average life, a life spent in enjoyment of the blisses of the commonplace:

"The condition to which some who have gone as far as you
Have succeeded in returning. They may remember
The vision they have had, but they cease to regret it,
Maintain themselves by the common routine,
Learn to avoid excessive expectation,
Become tolerant of themselves and others,
Giving and taking, in the usual actions
What there is to give and take. They do not repine;
Are contented with the morning that separates
And with the evening that brings together
For casual talk before the fire
Two people who know they do not understand each other,
Breeding children whom they do not understand
And who will never understand them."

Celia, as well she might, objects that this leaves her cold, that it seems a kind of surrender; although she is willing to admit that her reluctance to accept it might be a symptom of her illness, which is, of course, the malaise of an inauthentic existence. But Sir Henry — and it is difficult to tell here if he is acting as priest or psychoanalyst — tells her:

"There is another way, if you have the courage.
The first way I could describe in familiar terms
Because you have seen it, as we all have seen it,
Illustrated, more or less, in lives of those about us.
The second is unknown, and so requires faith —
The kind of faith that issues from despair.
The destination cannot be described;
You will know very little until you get there;
You will journey blind. But the way leads towards possession
Of what you have sought for in the wrong place."
Celia. "That sounds like what I want. But what is my duty?"
Reilly. "Whichever way you choose will prescribe its own
            duty."
Celia. "Which way is better?"
Reilly. "Neither way is better
            Both ways are necessary. It is also necessary
            To make a choice between them."

One is again reminded of Jean-Paul Sartre's admonition that man *must* choose his life: that is, he must decide the kind of person he is going to be, for when he says that man is condemned to be free, that is at least a part of what he means.

Celia chooses the second way; she becomes a nursing nun in Africa where, during a plague, she is crucified near an anthill by the natives she has been trying to heal. This is the end that Sir Henry saw for her when he echoed the prophetic words "it is finished." And this should come as no surprise, for Mr. Eliot, as everyone knows, is a good and pious Christian, and his Celia Coplestone is simply following Christ's example — the imagery and symbolism of the play leave no doubt of this. Her death, which the others regard as a tragic waste, as "thrown away on a few dirty natives," and for which they blame themselves, is the

53

certain sign, not of her failure, but of her transcendent success as a person. Sir Henry makes this very clear:

". . . because you think her death was waste
You blame yourselves, and because you blame yourselves,
You think her life was wasted. *It was triumphant!*"

At least Sir Henry Harcourt-Reilly, be he priest or psychiatrist, has recognized that Celia, of all the characters in the play, has the only life worth living. But Edward Chamberlayne is still uneasy about her sacrifice:

". . . if this was right— if this was right for Celia,
There must be something else that is terribly wrong
And the rest of us are somehow involved in the wrong."

What this wrong is is implicit throughout the entire play: it is the wrong of the empty, futile, and meaningless lives lived by most of us—the wrong which makes Celia's sacrifice necessary. It is, as the existentialist Heidegger, or the existential psychoanalyst Erich Fromm would put it, the wrong of the inauthentic existence which is the prevailing spiritual disease of our world— a disease which nothing short of this will cure. It is the wrong which is so oppressively familiar in Arthur Miller's disturbing play, *The Death of a Salesman.*

As compared with Mr. Eliot's two plays, *The Death of a Salesman* cannot be called a more serious play, but it is certainly a far more disturbing one. Willy Loman, the Salesman, is a figure of major proportions when held against the midgets who people Eliot's plays. For all the terrible significance of her experience, and the eternal quality of her sacrificial death, the substance of Celia Coplestone, it seems to me, would not fill a cavity in one of Willy Loman's teeth. But such comparisons are always unfair in these matters, and they only reflect the bias, ignorance, and ineptitude of the one who makes them. All three plays are excellent of their kind; it is only that my preference is solidly for Mr. Miller's play, although I am profoundly convinced that all three have much to teach us.

come a reality. Such childish whistling in the dark is an earnest solicitation for the deepest kind of trouble. This superficial optimism, which I believe we have shed, or are now in the process of shedding, is just what Spengler has called it — cowardice.

If we have learned nothing else in the present crisis, we have learned that corrupt dreams such as Willy's will not sustain even the least of us. As a result, we are no longer so certain as we once were that God is in his heaven, while, at the same time, we are quite certain that all is not right with the world. I think that if we keep in mind who we are (and I do *not* mean the invincible, God-chosen defenders of the divine right of property and free enterprise), and if we do our best to live the kind of lives we were intended to live, there is a great deal to be said for the future.

The one thing we cannot take for granted is that everything is going to be all right, nor, on the other hand, that calamity is inevitable. This is the same as saying that no matter what I do, things will turn out the same and nothing I can do will alter them. This means that I regard myself as a being of no significance, which is a very dangerous assumption to make — witness Willy Loman's tragic end. In fact, we must do just the opposite if we follow the examples which our playwrights have set before us. They have warned us three times that we must choose our own destiny, and a destiny in keeping with our highest hopes and aspirations, if we want to live anything but empty and meaningless lives in an empty and meaningless world. And this choice implies an earnest and ceaseless struggle to become a real person; that is, the kind of significant being which is worthy of making a choice which will influence the future of mankind. If we choose irresponsibly, believing that our choices do not matter, we can only degrade mankind and intensify the misery of our own existence. Even those who believe we have no freedom to choose, or who refuse to choose at all, have made choices — the choice of not choosing. Sooner or later we must all learn, like John Proctor in Arthur Miller's play, *The Crucible*, that even though all we have left in the end is our name, there is still a greater tragedy than merely dying, the tragedy of never having embraced our human freedom.

Of course I do not believe that it is necessary for all of us to follow John Proctor to the gallows to prove that at least we are men, and that there is "a little good in us." But I do think that we can all remember what it is that these authors have attempted to convey to us: that God intended something good when he made man; that he intended some unique good when he made each one of us; and that it is our only hope that we find out what this unique intention is and do our best to fulfill it. We may find, of course, that we have embarked upon a perilous journey, but after all this is our only hope for salvation. As I see it, we must learn to live authentically, or we will not live at all; we must choose the good that is in us, or be engulfed in the evils which surround us. And this, perhaps, more than anything I have said, reveals the simple message which the authors of modern literature, as well as the philosophers of existentialism, are trying so desperately to bring to our attention.